Percy Bysshe Shelley, Thomas James Wise

Poems and Sonnets

Percy Bysshe Shelley, Thomas James Wise

Poems and Sonnets

ISBN/EAN: 9783337006327

Printed in Europe, USA, Canada, Australia, Japan

Cover: Foto ©Thomas Meinert / pixelio.de

More available books at **www.hansebooks.com**

Poems and Sonnets.

BY

PERCY BYSSHE SHELLEY

EDITED

BY CHARLES ALFRED SEYMOUR

Philadelphia:

PRINTED FOR PRIVATE CIRCULATION ONLY.

1887.

CONTENTS.

PREFACE.

THE *Poems and Sonnets* ~~which compose~~ the following pages are reprinted verbatim from the first volume of Professor Dowden's *Life of Shelley*, published in London, England, by Messrs. Kegan Paul, Trench, and Co., in November last. They appear to have been written by Shelley at intervals during the years 1810—1814, and in all probability many of them were intended by him to be included in one volume with *Queen Mab*.[1] Whilst staying in Dublin he had placed in the hands of a printer of that town named Stockdale (not to be confounded with John Stockdale, Junior, of Pall Mall, the publisher of *St. Irvyne* and *Original Poetry by Victor and Cazire*) a manuscript volume of verse, and this manuscript volume, after his arrival in England, he made several attempts to recover—attempts which apparently proved ineffectual to secure its restoration. However, whether he succeeded

---

[1] "You will receive *Queen Mab* with the other poems," wrote Shelley to Hookham on February 19th, 1813 ; "I think that the whole should form one volume." There is, I imagine, but little doubt that the "other poems" of which Hookham is here advised are included in the manuscript collection of which the present series forms a part.

or not in regaining possession of his Dublin verse,
certain it is that during the closing months of his
life with Harriet he prepared for press a volume of
poetry, and it seems most probable that but for the
final rupture with Harriet and his flight with Mary
Godwin, Shelley would, between 1813, when he printed
Queen Mab, and 1816, when he published *Alastor*, have
added one more to the already ~~authorous tale~~ of literary
ventures with which his youthful muse favoured an
unappreciative world. Of the light in which Shelley
viewed his poetical work at this period we have abundant
evidence.[1] "My poems," he had written to Hookham
(January 2nd, 1813), "will, I fear, little stand the
criticism even of friendship; some of the latter ones
[perhaps *Queen Mab* is included in this reference] have
the merit of conveying a meaning in every word, and
all are faithful pictures of my feelings at the time of
writing them. But they are in a great measure abrupt
and obscure—all breathing hatred to government and
religion, but, I think, not too openly for publication. One
fault they are indisputably exempt from, that of being
a volume of *fashionable literature*. I doubt not but your
friendly hand will clip the wings of my Pegasus
considerably."

Hookham can scarcely have failed to discern in many
of these poems, in addition to that youthful ardor and

[1] See Dowden's *Life of Shelley*, vol. i., p. 344.
[1] "Two leaves," states Professor Dowden, "have unhappily been torn
away; otherwise the volume is in excellent condition."

enthusiasm which are most characteristic of Shelley at
that period, a great deal of vigor and originality ; but,
as I have said, the sudden change in Shelley's
domestic affairs, and his hurried departure for the
Continent, doubtless put for the time being all thoughts
of the publication of his poetical efforts out of his head.
Leaving Harriet, he left with her the book into
which (from first or early drafts) he had transcribed the
poems intended to form the contents of the projected
volume. This book, so far as the evidence at present
before us serves to show, he never reclaimed, and it has
accordingly remained in the hands of Harriet's descend-
ants to this day, and is at present in the possession
of Mr. C. J. E. Esdaile, by whose permission Professor
Dowden noticed it in his *Life of Shelley*, and there gave
from it those pieces which I now print in a collective form.

The following passages, descriptive of the contents of this
manuscript book, I give in Professor Dowden's own words.

" With the exception of five short pieces, subsequently
added by Harriet, the poems are in Shelley's handwriting; up to the point where the collection designed
for publication by Hookham closes, the lines were counted
by Shelley (not without a characteristic error in reckon-
ing), and the total number, as given by him (2,822) agrees
closely with the estimate furnished to Hookham in his
letter of January 26th, 1813.

" Of the shorter poems several may be described as
occasional. Several are direct inspirations—never trans-
scripts—from external nature, and seek to render into
words some of the emotion caused by its beauty, or

D

wonder, or terror. Now it is an exquisite spring day,
with influence felt in the nerves and in the blood as a
keen yet universal thrill of desire and delight; now
a day of late winter, which seems to anticipate the vernal
rapture, yet is fated to be pursued and defeated by
tempest and rains. Or Shelley is alone amid the ~~awful~~
desolation of the hills, and would fain confront the
awful spirit of the wild, waste places. Or he wanders
forth on the Sabbath morning, away from the church
and church-goers, through On a mountain labyrinth of
loveliness,' meditating on the worship and religion of
'the man sincerely good,' to whom every day is a
sabbath day :—

> " 'Consigned to thoughts of holiness,
>   And deeds of living love.'

Or he bends over a poison-berried plant, fair in leaf
and stem, and moralizes it into many meanings. Or the
sea wind blows on his breast and in his hair, and he
prolongs his pleasure by transmuting it into the gladness
of an imagined lover waiting for the breeze to blow her
true love to her arms. Other poems express the ardour of
his affection for Harriet, and in these there is a spiritual
quality not always to be found in poetry which tells of
the passion of boy and girl. She who is dear to him
can be dear only because she is his purer soul, and the
meeting of eyes, the touch of lips, are precious because
these are occasions and emblems of the union of two
ardent spirits panting together after high ends. In con-
trast with such hymns of love as those, Shelley sings of the
savage solitude and isolation of the wretch who cannot
love his fellows :—

> " 'Not the swarth Pariah in some Indian grove,
>   Lone, loan, and hunted by his brothers' hate,
>   Hath drunk so deep the cup of bitter fate.'

"And his own sympathies flow forth at the thought of the wrongs and woes of men; at the imagined sight of womanhood in anguish and despair; or at some tale from real life of the sorrows of the oppressed poor.[1] Or he contemplates the saviours and the destroyers of human happiness, those whose strength has been given to bless or to ban their kind—the warrior, the conqueror, the tyrant, and over against these the patriot-martyr by whose grave he muses. Or he sings a chant of freedom, and heartens himself against the fall of the champions of righteousness by the faith that death, which subdues all else, is powerless against virtue, truth, and love. Or he gazes into the future, expecting in the darkest midnight of doubt and fear a sudden dayspring :—

> " ' Then may we hope the consummating hour,
> Dreadfully, swiftly, sweetly, is arriving,
> When light from darkness, peace from desolation,
> Bursts unresisted.'

" Or his gaze reverts to the past, and he sees Desolation and Oblivion dwelling in the ruined palaces of mighty kings, and draws from the silence and horror auguries of solemn hope. Two narrative poems of considerable length exhibit Shelley at work on material which needs a firmer and calmer hand than his in early years to fashion it into forms of beauty; yet each contains some

---

[1] " *A Tale of Society as it is from Facts*, 1811, of which a fragment has been printed, is given in full in Shelley's manuscript. It also gives the complete translation of *La Marseillaise*, of which one stanza has been printed from a letter to Edward Graham. Having copied his best short pieces, Shelley falls back on the Oxford poems suggested by the story of Hogg's friend, Mary, and on the pieces written in the winter of 1810-11, which are strikingly inferior both in form and feeling to the poems of a later date."

well-wrought stanzas. *Henry and Louisa*, a poem in two
parts, with the motto, 'She died for love, and he for
glory,' is a tale of war, and in passing from the first to the
second part, the scene changes from England to the
Egyptian battle-field. Henry, borne from his lover's arms
by the insane lust of conquest and of glory, is pursued
by Louisa, who finds him dying on the bloody sands, and,
like Shakespeare's Juliet, is swift to pursue her beloved
through the portals of the grave. 'The stanza of this
poem,' wrote Shelley in a note, 'is radically that of
Spenser, although I suffered myself at the time of writing
it to be led into occasional deviations.' *Zeinab and
Kathema*, a poem in six-line stanzas, is also a tragedy
of love and death, very crude and ghastly-grotesque in
some of its details. In the summer of 1811 Shelley had
read with great admiration Miss Owenson's novel, *The
Missionary*. From this may have come the suggestion
to choose, as the heroine of his poem, a maiden of
Cashmire, borne away from her native home by Christian
guile and rapine. Kathema follows his betrothed Zeinab
to England :—

> " ' Meanwhile thro' calm and storm, thro' night and day,
>   Unvarying in her aim the vessel went,
>   As if some inward spirit ruled her way
>   And her tense sails were conscious of intent,
>   Till Albion's cliffs gleamed o'er her plunging bow,
>   And Albion's river-floods bright sparkled round her prow.'

"But Zeinab had been flung to perish upon the streets
by her betrayers, had risen in crime against those who
caused her ruin, and had suffered death by the vengeance
of indiscriminating and pitiless laws. It is a bitter
December evening when Kathema, weary with vain
search for his beloved, sinks wearily upon the heath. At
the moment of his awaking the winter moonbeams fall

upon a dead and naked female form, swinging in chains
from a gibbet, while her dark hair tosses in the wind, and
ravenous birds of prey cry in the ear of night. The lover
recognises his Zeinab, and is seized with madness; he
scales the gibbet, and, twining the chains around his
neck, leaps forward 'to meet the life to come.' Here is
romantic ghastliness, as imagined by a boy, in extravagant
profusion; but at heart each of the two poems is designed
less as a piece of romantic art than as an indictment of
wide-spread evils—the one, a setting forth of the criminal
lust of glory and conquest; the other, a setting forth of
the cruelty of sensual passion and the injustice of formally
administered laws. A soliloquy of that ancient outcast
and undying martyr, the Wandering Jew, brings to a close
the gathering of pieces intended for Hookham's considera-
tion. We trace in these early poems influences in various
degrees, derived from Southey, Campbell, Wordsworth,
Scott. The collection, which is introduced by the dedication to Harriet afterwards prefixed to *Queen Mab* (and
here given with some differences of phrasing), opens with
a series of poems in unrhymed stanzas, the use of which
Shelley learnt from Southey's early volumes. . . . Besides
the dedication, one other poem was transferred to *Queen
Mab* from this manuscript book—the dialogue between
Falsehood and Vice, which Shelley gave in a note to
Queen Mab, intimating that it was there printed because
it expressed strongly his abhorrence of despotism and
falsehood, and no other opportunity would probably occur
of rescuing it from oblivion. We may infer that when
the sheets of *Queen Mab* were going through the press
Shelley had already abandoned his intention of printing
the shorter pieces. One of these, and only one, appeared
subsequently with his sanction—that which expresses
with subtle power the sense of mystery which belongs

B

to man's life and death, and exhorts us to endure the
mystery courageously; the poem opening with the
lines :—

> "The pale, the cold, and the moony smile
> Which the meteor beam of a stormy night
> Sheds on a lonely and sea-girt isle
> Till the dawning of morn's undoubted light,
> Is the flame of life so fickle and wan
> That flits round our steps till their strength is gone.'

"This, with a revised text, formed one of the sheaf of
poems which accompanied *Alastor* into the world [see
Alastor, 1816 edition, pp. 61-63]; and Shelley's good
judgment appeared in his selection of this from his early
pieces, for it certainly touches a higher level than any
other of those which preceded *Queen Mab*." [1]

Professor Dowden might have gone further; for in
some respects the little poem excels almost any passage of
like bulk in *Queen Mab*. But I have not yet exhausted
the biographer's account of this volume of Shelley's early
poetic labors, on which he has had the honor of enlightening the public. Mr. Dowden says :—

"At Nantgwilt, in wooded glen or mountain solitude, or
in the company of voiceful streams, the poet cast off his
nightmare and awoke. Besides *The Retrospect*, several
unpublished pieces would seem to have been inspired by
the beauty, not untouched by awe and terror, of wild
Wales.[2] The poetical mood was not likely to pass away
when Shelley found himself at Lynmouth, still amid hills
and rushing brooks, and now in presence of the ever-
changing sea. It was certainly at Lynmouth, and in

---

[1] *Life of Shelley*, vol. I., pp. 345-349.
[2] "Some of these, however," adds Professor Dowden in a footnote,
"may belong to Shelley's visit of 1811."

August, 1812, that Shelley, stirred to creation by the mystery and music of the waves, wrote a fragment of some three hundred lines—still in manuscript—entitled *The Voyage*. It tells, in the irregular unrhymed verse which Shelley adopted from *Thalaba* and employed in *Queen Mab*, of a ship returning across the summer sea from her voyage; and of her company of voyagers with their various passions and imaginings—two ardent youths who have braved all dangers side by side; the landsman mean and crafty, who bears across the stainless ocean all the base thoughts and selfish greeds of the city; the sailor returning to his cottage-home, and wife and babes, but seized at the moment of his dearest hope by minions of the press-gang and hurried away reluctant.[1] Here also on the Devon coast was probably written *A Retrospect of Times of Old*—a rhymed piece, also unpublished, having much in common with those earlier pages of *Queen Mab*,[2] which picture the fall of empires, and celebrate the oblivion that has overtaken the old rulers of men and lords of the earth."[3]

Such is Professor Dowden's account of the series of poems which it has been his good fortune to bring to

[1] "*The Voyage*, like *Queen Mab*, passes before its close from the unrhymed Southean verse into blank verse."—(Note by Professor Dowden.)

[2] "In form," writes Professor Dowden, "*Queen Mab* agrees with *The Voyage*; in substance it has kinship with *A Retrospect of Times of Old*. It possesses a visionary largeness which corresponds with the mood into which the sea and the mountain solitudes had lifted Shelley's spirit. It is a kind of synthesis which harmonises the political and social fervors of the Irish expedition, with all their wisdom and unwisdom, and the imaginative exaltation to which the grandeur and loveliness of Welsh hillsides and the Devon cliffs and waves had given rise."

[3] *Life of Shelley*, vol. I, pp 284, 235. On page 293 of the same volume Professor Dowden states in a footnote that, "in a note to his poem, *The Voyage*, Shelley speaks of the purer generosity and more engaging frankness found in small trading vessels than those of the seamen of the Royal Navy.

the notice of the public—a series of great importance
to students of the growth of Shelley's genius. When we
remember the extreme puerility of Shelley's juvenile essays
in the poetic art, so far as they are at present known to
us, it is matter for astonishment to those who are best
acquainted with his work, that essays exhibiting so much
skill both in workmanship and design as some of these
(more especially some of the sonnets) do, should have
been produced by the poet during the years in question.
As Mr. Buxton Forman truly says,[1] "between *Queen Mab*
and *Alastor* there is a great gulf fixed," and now these
manuscripts appear to aid us in bridging the gulf.[2] They
show that Shelley attained perfection—granting that *Alastor*
is perfection, as I take it that it is, or nearly—at no one
bound, as has hitherto appeared, and prove that it was by
the exercise of patient care and continued labour that he
attained to that skill in his craft which is so characteristic
even of his early maturity. Were it for no other reason
than to portray the gradual but decided development of
his genius the publication in full of these poems would
be a matter of urgent necessity. By many it has been
understood that during these years (1812—1815) poetry
was comparatively neglected by Shelley, except for the
time devoted to the composition and revision of *Queen
Mab*. We now see clearly the error of such a surmise,
and can conceive how largely thought and patience were

---

[1] Shelley's *Works*, "Library" edition, 1882; vol. ∧ p. ∧ .
[2] These remarks apply, of course, to such of the poems as were written
during the period which elapsed between the composition of *Queen Mab*
and *Alastor*.

expended upon the cultivation of poesy in the intervals
of work for social and theological reform.

But there is another reason still why complete publication should be no longer delayed. Like the bulk of Shelley's poetry, these sonnets are reflections of himself, and exhibit most clearly and vividly the various phases of his character, and more particularly his feelings—latterly gradually, almost imperceptibly, changing—towards his wife during the years over which the series extends. His views upon various social problems are also rendered more visibly apparent; and the development of his imaginative faculty, as well as his technical and artistic skill, is abundantly evidenced. Clearly the interests of the biographer, equally with those of the critic, call loudly for their full and prompt appearance; and in the meantime it is much more convenient to have the published poems and fragments brought together in a volume, than scattered through the pages of a bulky *Life of Shelley.*

Such are the reasons which have induced me—pending the publication of the remainder—to print at once such examples of the whole as Professor Dowden has incorporated in his great work. As soon as that work reached this country I applied to several of our leading publishers, and earnestly entreated them to publish the selections, but, with a consideratenoss for English interests in the book, quite new in these States, and one and all declined.[1] I

---

[1] I confess I cannot understand this squeamishness. As long as no international copyright treaty exists, every American has a right to print English literature, as every Englishman has to print American literature.

F

back

had no option, therefore, but to adopt the only remaining
course and to print them privately, and this I have done
without loss of time.   The number produced is—I venture
to think, advisedly—extremely limited, my desire being
simply and solely to place in the hands of known Shelley
students on either side of the Atlantic these specimens of
the youthful poet's growing power which, in a handy and
connected form, cannot fail to be of service to them.

1/

   The Wandering Jew's Soliloquy (pp.   ) was not
given by Professor Dowden, who contented himself by
merely stating that such a -piece was included in the
manuscript volume (see *ante*, p.).   The poem first
appeared in an edition of *The Wandering Jew* issued a
few weeks since by the English Shelley Society/where it
was printed—as a footnote appended to it informs us—by
Mr. Esdaile's express permission.

17/

2/

al]

   It only remains to add that in preparing the present
book I have printed the ~~various~~ poems precisely as they
are given by Professor Dowden, and have included in
the form of footnotes whatever remarks he makes regard-
ing the various individual pieces.   In this preface, also,
I have obtruded myself as little as possible, and have
sought rather to give by the use of the Professor's own
words as clear and concise an idea of the whole as was
possible.   Any additional comments of my own would
have been both needless and out of place, and would have
served, probably, to mystify rather than to enlighten.   The

X

When we have such a treaty, that right will no longer exist.   Such a
print as the present will then be illegal; and I, for one, would not think
liberty best served by breaking the law.—C.A.S.

editing of the little book has been conducted with the most
anxious care, and the typography executed in the most
skilful manner. The thirty copies of which the edition
consists have been printed upon Whatman's hand-made
paper, which I have obtained from England especially for
the purpose.

CHARLES ALFRED SEYMOUR.

PHILADELPHIA,
April 1st, 1887.

It is, I suppose, hardly necessary to add that not one of these thirty copies will at any time, or in any manner, be offered for sale. The majority of them will be placed in the principle public libraries where they will be at all times accessible to any who may desire to peruse them. The few remaining will be gratuitously presented by myself to such recognized Shelley specialists (both here in the States and in England) as are most likely to appreciate them, and to derive pleasure or profit from their possession.

POEMS AND SONNETS. ✗

G

TO HARRIET * * * *.

Whose is the love that, gleaming through the world,
Wards off the poisonous arrow of its scorn?
    Whose is the warm and partial praise
    Virtue's most sweet reward?

Beneath whose looks did my reviving soul
Riper in truth and virtuous daring grow?
    Whose eyes have I gazed fondly on,
    And loved mankind the more?

Harriet! on thine:—thou wert my purer mind;
Thou wert the inspiration of my song;
    Thine are these early wilding flowers,
    Though garlanded by me.

Then press unto thy breast this pledge of love;
And know, though time may change and years may roll,
    Each floweret gather'd in my heart
    It consecrates to thine.

POEMS AND SONNETS.

THE RETROSPECT: CWM ELAN, 1812.[1]

" A scene which wildered fancy viewed
In the soul's coldest solitude,
With that same scene when peaceful love
Flings rapture's colour o'er the grove,
When mountain, meadow, wood, and stream
With unalloying glory gleam,
And to the spirit's ear and eye
Are unison and harmony.
The moonlight was my dearer day;

[1] " ' Nantgwilt, the place where we now reside,' wrote Shelley to Godwin (April 25, 1812), ' is in the neighbourhood of scenes marked deeply on my mind by the thoughts which possessed it when present among them. The ghosts of these old friends have a dim and strange appearance, when resuscitated in a situation so altered as mine is, since I felt that they were alive.' There was, indeed, a wide difference between this nestling into the green valley, with Harriet by his side, and the solitary visit in the summer of 1811, when many causes conspired to render him dispirited, distraught, and at times oppressed with morbid gloom. As Shelley thought of this his feelings took shape in verse. In a poem, hitherto unprinted, existing in Shelley's handwriting, and entitled *The Retrospect: Cwm Elan*, 1812, he contrasts the Cwm Elan of 1811 with the same hills and vale and wood in these happier days of the ensuing spring."—Dowden's *Life of Shelley*, 1886, vol i. pp. 269, 270.

Then would I wander far away,
And, lingering on the wild brook's shore
To hear its unremitting roar,
Would lose in the ideal flow
All sense of overwhelming woe;
Or at the noiseless noon of night
Would climb some heathy mountain's height,
And listen to the mystic sound
That stole in fitful gasps around.
I joyed to see the streaks of day
Above the purple peaks decay,
And watch the latest line of light
Just mingling with the shades of night;
For day with me was time of woe
When even tears refused to flow;
Then would I stretch my languid frame
Beneath the wild wood's gloomiest shade,
And try to quench the ceaseless flame
That on my withered vitals preyed;
Would close mine eyes and dream I were
On some remote and friendless plain,
And long to leave existence there,
If with it I might leave the pain
That with a finger cold and lean
Wrote madness on my withering mien.

"It was not unrequited love

That bade my wildered spirit rove ;
'Twas not the pride disdaining life, .
That with this mortal world at strife
Would yield to the soul's inward sense,
Then groan in human impotence,
And weep because it is not given
To taste on Earth the peace of Heaven.
'Twas not that in the narrow sphere
Where nature fixed my wayward fate
There was no friend or kindred dear
Formed to become that spirit's mate,
Which, searching on tired pinion, found
Barren and cold repulse around ;
Oh no ! yet each one sorrow gave
New graces to the narrow grave.

" For broken vows had early quelled
The stainless spirit's vestal flame :
Yes ! whilst the faithful bosom swelled,
Then the envenoned arrow came,
And apathy's unaltering eye
Beamed coldness on the misery ;
And early I had learned to scorn
The chains of clay that bound a soul
Panting to seize the wings of morn,
And where its vital fires were born.

H.

To soar, and spurn the cold control
Which the vile slaves of earthly night
Would twine around its struggling flight.

" O many were the friends whom fame
Had linked with the unmeaning name,
Whose magic marked among mankind
The casket of my unknown mind,
Which hidden from the vulgar glare
Imbibed no fleeting radiance there.
My darksome spirit sought, it found
A friendless solitude around.
For who that might undaunted stand,
The saviour of a sinking land,
Would crawl, its ruthless tyrant's slave,
And fatten upon Freedom's grave,
Tho' doomed with her to perish, where
The captive clasps abhorred despair.

" They could not share the bosom's feeling,
Which, passion's every throb revealing,
Dared force on the world's notice cold
Thoughts of unprofitable mould,
Who bask in Custom's fickle ray,
Fit sunshine of such wintry day !
They could not in a twilight walk

Weave an impassioned web of talk,
Till mysteries the spirits press
In wild yet tender awfulness,
Then feel within our narrow sphere
How little, yet how great we are !
But they might shine in courtly glare,
Attract the rabble's cheapest stare,
And might command where'er they move
A thing that bears the name of love ;
They might be learned, witty, gay,
Foremost in fashion's gilt array,
On Fame's emblazoned pages shine,
Be princes' friends, but never mine !

" Ye jagged peaks that frown sublime,
Mocking the blunted scythe of Time,
Whence I would watch its lustre pale
Steal from the moon o'er yonder vale :

" Thou rock, whose bosom black and vast
Bared to the stream's unceasing flow,
Ever its giant shade doth cast
On the tumultuous surge below :

" Woods, to whose depth retires to die
The wounded echo's melody,

And whither this lone spirit bent
The footstep of a wild intent :

" Meadows ! whose green and spangled breast
These fevered limbs have often pressed,
Until the watchful fiend Despair
Slept in the soothing coolness there !
Have not your varied beauties seen
The sunken eye, the withering mien,
Sad traces of the unuttered pain
That froze my heart and burned my brain.

" How changed since nature's summer form.
Had last the power my grief to charm,
Since last ye soothed my spirit's sadness
Strange chaos of a mingled madness !
Changed !—not the loathsome worm that fed
In the dark mansions of the dead
Now soaring thro' the fields of air,
And gathering purest nectar there,
A butterfly, whose million hues
The dazzled eye of wonder views,
Long lingering on a work so strange,
Has undergone so bright a change.

" How do I feel my happiness ?
I cannot tell, but they may guess

Whose every gloomy feeling gone,
Friendship and passion feel alone ;
Who see mortality's dull clouds
Before affection's murmur fly,
Whilst the mild glances of her eye
Pierce the thin veil of flesh that shrouds
The spirit's inmost sanctuary.

" O thou ![1] whose virtues latest known,
First in this heart yet claim'st a throne ;
Whose downy sceptre still shall share
The gentle sway with virtue there ;
Thou fair in form, and pure in mind,
Whose ardent friendship rivets fast
The flowery band our fates that bind,
Which incorruptible shall last
When duty's hard and cold control
Had thawed around the burning soul ;
The gloomiest retrospects, that bind
With crowns of thorn the bleeding mind ;
The prospects of most doubtful hue,
That rise on Fancy's shuddering view ;
Are gilt by the reviving ray
Which thou hast flung upon my day."

[1] Harriet.

I

TO HARRIET.

IT is not blasphemy to hope that Heaven
More perfectly will give those nameless joys
Which throb within the pulses of the blood
And sweeten all that bitterness which Earth
Infuses in the heaven-born soul. O thou
Whose dear love gleamed upon the gloomy path
Which this lone spirit travelled, drear and cold,
Yet swiftly leading to those awful limits
Which mark the bounds of time and of the space
When Time shall be no more ; wilt thou not turn
Those spirit-beaming eyes and look on me,
Until I be assured that Earth is Heaven
And Heaven is Earth ?—will not thy glowing cheek,
Glowing with soft suffusion, rest on mine,
And breathe magnetic sweetness thro' the frame
Of my corporeal nature, thro' the soul,

[handwritten marginal and footnote annotations:]

... eight lines, from ... Whose dear love ...ed to And Heaven ...th, seem to have ...written out by Shelley ...t twice. A ...

*... in Shelley's handwriting exists amongst the "Boscombe MSS. * from which the ...e was copied by Dr Garnett. ... From Dr Garnett's ... transcript they ...printed by Mr Rossetti in his edition of Shelley's Works (Vol. iii, p. 365) whence 1880 they were again reprinted by Mr Forman (Shelley's Works, "Library" ..., Vol. iv, p. 359).*

Mr Codaile's manuscript volume must be recognized as 'clean copy' finally

Now knit with these fine fibres ? I would give
The longest and the happiest day that fate
Has marked on my existence but to feel'
One soul-reviving kiss. . . . O thou most dear,
'Tis an assurance that this Earth is Heaven,
And Heaven the flower of that untainted seed
Which springeth here beneath such love as ours.
Harriet ! let death all mortal ties dissolve,
But ours shall not be mortal ! The cold hand
Of Time may chill the love of earthly minds
Half frozen now ; the frigid intercourse
Of common souls lives but a summer's day ;
It dies, where it arose, upon this earth.
But ours ! oh, 'tis the stretch of fancy's hope
To portray its continuance as now,
Warm, tranquil, spirit-healing ; nor when age
Has tempered these wild extasies, and given
A soberer tinge to the luxurious glow,
Which blazing on devotion's pinnacle
Makes virtuous passion supersede the power
Of reason ; nor when life's æstival sun
To deeper manhood shall have ripened me ;
Nor when some years have added judgment's store
To all thy woman sweetness, all the fire
Which throbs in thine enthusiast heart ; not then
Shall holy friendship (for what other name

revised for press, the Boscombe version is in all probability an
early draft. The minute textual variations which it exhibits must
therefore in future be discarded in favor of the reading given
above.

May love like ours assume ?)/not even then
Shall custom so corrupt, or the cold forms
Of this desolate world so harden us,
As when we think of the dear love that binds
Our souls in soft communion, while we know
Each other's thoughts and feelings, can we say
Unblushingly a heartless compliment,
Praise, hate, or love with the unthinking world,
Or dare to cut the/relaxing nerve
That knits our love to Virtue. Can those eyes
Beaming with mildest radiance on my heart
To purify its purity, e'er bend
To sooth its vice or consecrate its fears ?
Never, thou second self! Is confidence
So vain in virtue that I learn to doubt
The mirror even of Truth ? Dark flood of Time,
Roll as it listeth thee ; I measure not
By months or moments thy ambiguous course.
Another may stand by me on thy brink,
And watch the bubble whirled beyond his ken,
Which pauses at my feet. The sense of love,
The thirst for action, and the impassioned thought
Prolong my being ; if I wake no more,
My life more actual living will contain
Than some grey veterans of the world's cold school,
Whose listless hours unprofitably roll

These twelve lines, from "Dark flood of Time" to "By one enthusiast
cling unredeemed", were given by Shelley (with one or two minute
variations) in one of his voluminous Notes to Queen Mab. (See Queen Mab,
13 edition, p. 210.)

By one enthusiast feeling unredeemed.

Virtue and Love! unbending Fortitude,

Freedom, Devotedness, and Purity!

That life my spirit consecrates to you." [1]

---

[1] " In Mr. Esdaile's manuscript book this poem immediately precedes the Sonnet to Harriet on August 1, 1812. The reader cannot fail to note that this poem contains several reminiscences of Wordsworth's *Tintern Abbey*, which it resembles in the general treatment of the blank verse. It occurs to me as possible that, in passing through Chepstow, Shelley may have visited Tintern Abbey, and have read Wordsworth's poem, and that this may have been written soon after reaching Lynmouth. Undoubtedly he had read the *Lyrical Ballads* at Keswick." (Note by Professor DOWDEN)

Life of Shelley, Vol. i, p. 288.

[See post, p. 57.]

SONNET.

TO A BALLOON LADEN WITH KNOWLEDGE.[1]

BRIGHT ball of flame that thro' the gloom of even
   Silently takest thine ethereal way,
   And with surpassing glory dimm'st each ray
Twinkling amid the dark blue depths of Heaven,—
Unlike the fire thou bearest, soon shalt thou
   Fade like a meteor in surrounding gloom,
Whilst that unquenchable is doomed to glow
   A watch-light by the patriot's lonely tomb;
A ray of courage to the opprest and poor;
   A spark, though gleaming on the hovel's hearth,
Which through the tyrant's gilded domes shall roar;
   A beacon in the darkness of the Earth;
A sun which, o'er the renovated scene,
Shall dart like Truth where Falsehood yet has been.

[1] The "Knowledge" of this and the following Sonnet consisted, of course, of copies of such elevating and enlightening literature as *An Address to the Irish People, Proposals for an Association of Philanthropists,* and the broadside *Declaration of Rights,* literature which, it will be remembered, Shelley took such original and unusual means for publishing. Were it only for the earnestness they exhibit as lying at the bottom of an apparently puerile and Quixotic enterprise, these *Sonnets* would be of the utmost interest and value.

SONNET.

ON LAUNCHING SOME BOTTLES FILLED WITH KNOWLEDGE
INTO THE BRISTOL CHANNEL.

VESSELS of heavenly medicine ! may the breeze
  Auspicious waft your dark green forms to shore ;
  Safe may ye stem the wide surrounding roar
Of the wild whirlwinds and the raging seas ;
And oh ! if Liberty e'er deigned to stoop
  From yonder lowly throne her crownless brow,
Sure she will breathe around your emerald group
  The fairest breezes of her west that blow.
Yes ! she will waft ye to some free-born soul
  Whose eye-beam kindling as it meets your freight,
  Her heaven-born flame in suffering Earth will light,
Until its radiance gleams from pole to pole,
  And tyrant-hearts with powerless envy burst
  To see their night of ignorance dispersed.

ON LEAVING LONDON FOR WALES.[1]

["This poem," writes Professor Dowden, "of eight
stanzas, of which I print four by permission of Mr.
Esdaile, is entitled *On Leaving London for Wales.*
Expressions in the piece seem to show that it was not
written actually in presence of the Welsh landscape. It
can only refer to the present occasion, or to the visit
in 1811 to Cwm Elan. In all respects—including the
reference to Snowdon — it seems to me to suit the
autumn of 1812 better than the summer of 1811."]

"HAIL to thee, Cambria! for the unfettered wind
Which from thy wilds even now methinks I feel,
Chasing the clouds that roll in wrath behind,
And tightening the soul's laxest nerves to steel;

[1] "It was a joy to Shelley to escape from the excitement and hurry of
the great city, with its painfully contrasted extremes of wealth and
misery, to the free air and joyous strength of the hills. Yet he had
dedicated himself to the service of man rather than to the worship of
nature; if virtue flowed into him from mountain and vale, this must
nerve him to renewed effort on behalf of his toiling and suffering fellows,
and by its calming influence must chasten and purify the indignation
which seized him at sight of the wrongs and outrages endured by the
wretched and the oppressed. Such thoughts and feelings as these took
shape in a poem, written perhaps in anticipation of his departure from

True mountain Liberty alone may heal
The pain which Custom's obduracies bring,
And he who dares in fancy even to steal
One draught from Snowdon's ever sacred spring
Blots out the unholiest rede of worldly witnessing.

"And shall that soul, to selfish peace resigned,
So soon forget the woe its fellows share ?
Can Snowdon's Lethe from the freeborn mind
So soon the page of injured penury tear ?
Does this fine mass of human passion dare
To sleep, unhonouring the patriot's fall,
Or life's sweet load in quietude to bear
While millions famish even in Luxury's hall,
And Tyranny high raisèd, stern, lowers on all ?

"No, Cambria ! never may thy matchless vales
A heart so false to hope and virtue shield ;
Nor ever may thy spirit-breathing gales
Waft freshness to the slaves who dare to yield.
For me ! . . . the weapon that I burn to wield
I seek amid thy rocks to ruin hurled,

London, in which he breathes a farewell to the 'miserable city,' with its
dark tide of woe and glare of loveless mirth, and then looks forth with
desire towards the wild Welsh hills."—(DOWDEN's *Life of Shelley*, 1886,
vol. ɣ, p. 317.)

That Reason's flag may over Freedom's field,
Symbol of bloodless victory, wave unfurled,
A meteor-sign of love effulgent o'er the world.

"Do thou, wild Cambria, calm each struggling thought,
Cast thy sweet veil of rocks and woods between,
That, by the soul to indignation wrought
Mountains and dells be mingled with the scene;
Let me for ever be what I have been,
But not for ever at my needy door
Let Misery linger speechless, pale, and lean;
I am the friend of the unfriended poor,
Let me not madly stain their righteous cause in gore."

SONNET.

TO IANTHE: SEPTEMBER, 1813.[1]

I LOVE thee, Baby! for thine own sweet sake :
Those azure eyes, that faintly dimpled cheek,
Thy tender frame so eloquently weak,
Love in the sternest heart of hate might wake ;
But more when o'er thy fitful slumber bending,
Thy mother folds thee to her wakeful heart, ,
Whilst love and pity in her glances blending,

[1] "The early summer of 1813 had been bleak and churlish ; flowers opened timidly and late, and fruits were harsh and crude. But before June was over a new brightness had entered the year for Shelley and Harriet—a little, fair, blue-eyed babe was born. By the twenty-eighth of the month the young mother was rapidly recovering. They named the blue-eyed girl Ianthe—'Violet-blossom.'—a comer to redeem the broken promises of spring ; the name, known to readers of Ovid, was also that given by Shelley to the first daughter of his imagination, the violet-eyed lady of *Queen Mab.* They added the name of Elizabeth. It doubtless pleased Harriet that the child should be called after her sister, and Shelley's favourite sister was an Elizabeth. 'This accession to his family,' says Hogg, 'did not appear to afford Shelley any gratification or to create an interest. He never spoke of his child to me.' And Harriet, Hogg goes on to say, was unwilling to let him see the little one, because the child suffered from some trivial blemish in one of her eyes ; and the mother, herself a beauty, could not bear that it should be known that one so nearly

All that thy passive eyes can feel impart :
More, when some feeble lineaments of her
Who bore thy weight beneath her spotless bosom,
As with deep love I read thy face, recur ;
More dear art thou, O fair and fragile blossom ;
Dearest when most thy tender traits express
The image of thy mother's loveliness.

connected with her was not perfectly beautiful. From which we learn that Shelley and Harriet did not turn to Hogg—'a pearl within an oyster shell'[1]—for sympathy in their new joy. We know that Harriet delighted in the babe's azure eyes, and that Shelley had a father's happiness in fondling and cherishing his fragile blossom of humanity. 'He was extremely fond of his child,' writes Peacock, 'and would walk up and down a room with it in his arms for a long time together, singing to it a monotonous melody of his own making, which ran on the repetition of a word of his own making. His song was ' Yâhmani, Yâhmani, Yâhmani, Yâhmani.[2] It did not please me, but, what was more important, it pleased the child, and lulled it to sleep when it was fretful. Shelley was extremely fond of his children. He was pre-eminently an affectionate father.' When Ianthe was three months old Shelley told his love for her and for her mother—two feelings now blended into one—in words of a dialect more familiar than that of his 'Yâhmani' song, which last was intelligible only to that now comer from the ante-natal world to whom it was crooningly addressed." —(Professor Dowden, *Life of Shelley*, 1886, vol. i. pp. 375, 376.)

_____

[1] " So Shelley describes Hogg in a letter to Mrs. Gisborne."
[2] " Peacock adds in a note : ' The tune was the uniform repetition of three notes, not very true in their intervals. The nearest resemblance will be found in the second, third, and fourth of a minor key : D, C, D, for example, in the key of A natural, a crotchet and two quavers.'"

SONNET.

EVENING. TO HARRIET.[1] X

O THOU bright Sun ! ' beneath the dark blue line
Of western distance that sublime descendest,
And gleaming lovelier as thy beams decline,
. Thy million hues to every vapour lendest,
.... And over cobweb lawn and grove and stream
Sheddest the liquid magic of thy light,
Till calm Earth, with the parting splendour bright,
Shows like the vision of a beauteous dream ;
What gazer now with astronomic eye
Could coldly count the spots within thy sphere ?
Such were thy lover, Harriet, could he fly
The thoughts of all that makes his passion dear,
And turning senseless from thy warm caress
Pick flaws in our close-woven happiness.

July 31st, 1813.

[1] "The sonnet to Ianthe, written in September, 1813, has told us how the babe was dear not only for its own sake but for the mother's, and how the mother had grown dearer for the babe's. A few days after the arrival of the Shelleys at Bracknell, Harriet completed her eighteenth year.

M

[See post, p. 57.]

Twelve months ago, at Lynmouth, Shelley had celebrated the anniversary in a sonnet bright in its confidence of ever-enduring love. Now, as the sun sank towards the far horizon, on the last evening of July, he thought wistfully, fondly, yet almost fearfully of his happiness with Harriet, whose birthday was on the morrow, and he expressed his feelings in a sonnet. In spite of its words of cheer, there is something in it of the strangeness and sadness of sunset; in the tone of its closing lines one detects already the little rift within the lover's lute, which had seemed to be healed, or never to have gaped at all, when the later and happier sonnet to Ianthe was written. . . . As yet, however, if there was a speck upon Shelley's happiness, it was no more than a speck; nor had Harriet cause for discontent. 'Very blooming and very happy,' she seemed to Mrs. Newton during the visit of the Newtons to High Elms. 'Ianthe,' adds that lady in a letter to Hogg, 'was grown surprisingly, and Miss Westbrook ever smiling and serene.'"—(Professor DOWDEN, *Life of Shelley*, 1886, vol. i, pp. 385, 386.)

---

[1] In the manuscript volume in Mr. Esdaile's possession this sonnet is headed (in Shelley's handwriting) "Sept. 1813"—'the date," supposes Professor Dowden, "of Shelley's copying the poem into the book, which probably had been given to Harriet. At the close is the date of composition —'July 31st, 1813.'"

TO HARRIETT :[1] MAY, 1814.[2]

Thy look of love has power to calm.
The stormiest passion of my soul ;
Thy gentle words are drops of balm
In life's too bitter bowl
No grief is mine, but that alone
These choicest blessings I have known.

[1] "The spelling of the name 'Harriett,'" says Professor Dowden, "is that of the manuscript, but was not usual with either Shelley or his wife in earlier days."

[2] "Early in May [1814] Shelley was in London. He did not yet despair of reconciliation with Harriet, nor had he ceased to love her. There is a tragic sonnet—one of the greatest in English poetry—by Michael Drayton, in which a lover, standing, as it were, by the death-bed of love, is heard bidding a passionate yet manly farewell to the joy and hope about to pass away for ever. And yet, until Death has set his seal on lips and brow, there cannot come the absolute blank of despair.

' Now at the last gasp of love's latest breath,
  When his pulse failing, passion speechless lies,
When faith is kneeling by his bed of death,
  And innocence is closing up his eyes,
—Now, if thou would'st, when all have given him over,
From death to life thou might'st him yet recover.'

Such a moment as this, and such a desperate hope as that uttered in Drayton's sonnet, find record in a poem addressed by Shelley to Harriet in May, 1814. It is the first of a few short pieces added in Harriet's hand-writing to the manuscript collection of poems prepared by Shelley for

Harriett ! if all who long to live

  In the warm sunshine of thine eye,

That price beyond all pain must give

  Beneath thy scorn to die—

Then hear thy chosen own too late [1]

His heart most worthy of thy-hate.

Be thou, then, one among mankind

  Whose heart is harder not for state,

Thou only virtuous, gentle, kind,

  Amid a world of hate ;

And by a slight endurance seal

A fellow-being's lasting weal.

publication in the early days of the preceding year. In this piteous appeal Shelley declares that he has now no grief but one—the grief of having known and lost his wife's love ; if it is the fate of all who would live in the sunshine of her affection to endure her scorn, then let him be scorned above the rest, for he most of all has desired that sunshine ; let not the world and the pride of life harden her heart ; it is better that she should be kind and gentle ; if she has something to endure, it is not much, and all her husband's weal hangs upon her loving endurance ; for, see how pale and wildered anguish has made him ; oh ! in mercy do not cure his malady by the fatal way of condemning him to exile beyond all hope or further fear ; oh I trust no erring guide, no unwise counsellor, no false pride ; rather learn that a nobler pride may find its satisfaction in and through love ; or if love be for ever dead, at least let pity survive in its room. . . . It is evident that in May, 1814, Harriet had assumed an attitude of hard alienation towards her husband, who pleaded with almost despairing hope for the restoration of her love."—(Professor Dowden, *Life of Shelley*, 1886, vol. i, pp. 412 (418.)

[1] *i.e.* "Then thy chosen one (thy husband) acknowledge too late that he most deserves thy hate because he has loved thee best."

For pale with anguish is his cheek,
  His breath comes fast, his eyes are dim,
Thy name is struggling ere he speak,
  Weak is each trembling limb;
In mercy let him not endure
The misery of a fatal cure.

O trust for once no erring guide
  Bid the remorseless feeling flee;
'Tis malice, 'tis revenge, 'tis pride,
  'Tis anything but thee;
O deign a nobler pride to prove,
And pity if thou canst not love.

COOK'S HOTEL.

MINOR FRAGMENTS.

MINOR FRAGMENTS.

THE TOMBS.

" ' We are now embosomed in the solitude of mountains, woods, and rivers,' wrote Shelley to Miss Hitchener,[1] ' silent, solitary, and old; far from any town; six miles from Rhyader, which is nearest. A ghost haunts the house, which has frequently been seen by the servants. We have several witches in our neighbourhood, and are quite stocked with fairies and hobgoblins of every description.' It was a fit home for a poet, and some of the feelings which had possessed Shelley during his visit to the Irish capital now took form in verse. Here, perhaps, was written a short unpublished poem entitled *The Tombs*, expressing a faith in the immortality of

> ' Courage and charity and truth
> And high devotedness,'

even in presence of the mouldering clay of the patriot's brain and heart, and amid the mournful emblems of the grave."

[1] Postmark, April 18, 1812.

o

ON ROBERT EMMET'S GRAVE.[1]

" No trump tells thy virtues—the grave where they rest
   With thy dust shall remain unpolluted by fame,
Till thy foes, by the world and by fortune carest,
   Shall pass like a mist from the light of thy name.

" When the storm-cloud that lowers o'er the day-beam is
      gone,
   Unchanged, unextinguished its lifespring will shine ;
When Erin has ceased with their memory to groan,
   She will smile through the tears of revival on thine." [2]

[1] The manuscript of this poem consists of *seven* stanzas, but only the
last *two* are given by Professor Dowden.
[2] "I have written some *verses* on Robert Emmet, which you shall see,
and which I will insert in my book of poems."—Shelley to Miss
Hitchiner ; Mac-Carthy's *Shelley's Early Life*, 1872, p. 134 (also p, 330.)
See also Dowden's *Life of Shelley*, 1886, Vol. 1, p. 268.

Cap.

The poem was probably at Nantgwillt,
about April, 1812.

TO HARRIET.

A BIRTHDAY SONNET.

"Among the strange books which Shelley had lately read was Sir James Lawrence's *Empire of the Nairs*, which convinced him, if any doubts yet remained, that marriage is essentially an evil. Having borrowed through Hookham a copy of Lawrence's poem, *Love/an Allegory*, he wrote to the author, and confessing that he had submitted for his wife's sake to the bondage of the marriage ceremony, added a graceful acknowledgment of his happiness: 'I am a young man not yet of age, and have now been married a year to a woman younger than myself. Love seems inclined to stay in the prison.' On the 1st of August came round Harriet's birthday, and Shelley addressed to her a birthday sonnet, confidently expecting for her a future of ardent love and pure thoughts like those of the present, however age might dim the light of her eyes or change her bright tresses to grey."

"Ever as now with Love and Virtue's glow
  May thy unwithering soul not cease to burn,
  Still may thine heart with those pure thoughts o'erflow
  Which force from mine such quick and warm return."

1. Professor Dowden, *Life of Shelley*, 1886, Vol. i, p. 286.

SONNET.

WRITTEN BEFORE LEAVING LYNMOUTH FOR ILFRACOMBE.

"In these August days [of 1812] Shelley doubtless
had a feeling that there was thunder in the upper
regions, and that the air might at any moment begin
to hurtle about his head. The quiet happiness of the
Lynmouth cottage was over and gone. Shelley had
loved to stand on the slope before his door, engaged in
the delightful pastime of blowing soap-bubbles, and
would watch the gleaming aërial voyagers until they
suddenly broke and vanished. The radiant summer
hours seemed to have disappeared like so many bright
bubbles borne away. He was impatient to be gone from
Devon, and to find a refuge across the Bristol Channel,
somewhere in his beloved Wales, possibly northwards in
the Vale of Llangollen, where, before these Barnstaple
troubles, he had planned to make his abode at least for
the coming winter. It was Shelley's design to sail from
Lynmouth to Swansea, a distance of about twenty-five
miles, but the winds of heaven refused to aid his flight.

d mt rt tct m 0

He breathed his longing for 'the south's benign and balmy breeze' in a sonnet, which signed, as it were, a farewell to the wilds of North Devon:—

+ 'Where man's profane and tainting hand
Nature's primeval loveliness has marred,
And some few souls of the high bliss debarred
Which else obey her powerful command;'

at the same time hailing from afar the

'Mountain piles
That load in grandeur Cambria's emerald vales.'

Still, however, the north wind blew, and he was defeated of his purpose. Unwilling to remain longer at Lynmouth, Shelley, with his household party and Miss Hitchener, towards the close of August, journeyed to Ilfracombe, and thence with little or no delay passed over to Swansea."

Indent

1. "The precise date of Shelley's departure is unascertained, but Godwin, writing from Lynmouth on September 19, states that he had been gone for three weeks." — Professor Dowden, Life of Shelley, 1886, Vol. i, p. 298-299.

-

LINES TO LIBERTY.[1]

"And the spirits of the brave
Shall start from every grave,
Whilst from her Atlantic throne
Freedom sanctifies the groan
That fans the glorious fires of its change

*   *   *   *   *   *

[1] "A direct reminiscence," says Professor Dowden, "from *Ye Mariners of England*, and *The Battle of the Baltic*."

Life of Shelley, Vol. i, p. 348

THE WANDERING JEW'S SOLILOQUY.

THE WANDERING JEW'S SOLILOQUY.

Is it the Eternal Triune, is it He
Who dares arrest the wheels of destiny
And plunge me in the lowest Hell of Hells?
Will not the lightning's blast destroy my frame?
Will not steel drink the blood-life where it swells?
No—let me hie where dark Destruction dwells,
To rouse her from her deeply caverned lair,
And taunting her curst sluggishness to ire·
Light long Oblivion's death torch at its flame
And calmly mount Annihilation's pyre.

Tyrant of Earth!. pale misery's jackal thou!
Are there no stores of vengeful violent fate
Within the magazines of thy fierce hate?
No poison in the clouds to bathe a brow
That lowers on thee with desperate contempt?
Where is the noonday pestilence that slew
The myriad sons of Israel's favoured nation?
Where the destroying minister that flew

Q

Pouring the fiery tide of desolation
Upon the leagued Assyrian's attempt?
Where the dark Earthquake demon who ingorged
At the dread word Korah's unconscious crew?
Or the Angel's two-edged sword of fire that urged
Our primal parents from their bower of bliss
(Reared by thine hand) for errors not their own
By Thine omniscient mind foredoomed, foreknown?
Yes! I would court a ruin such as this,
Almighty Tyrant! and give thanks to Thee—
Drink deeply—drain the cup of hate—remit this I
   may die.